NUTS

NUTS

NUTRITIOUS RECIPES WITH NUTS,
FROM SALTY OR SPICY TO SWEET

This edition published by Parragon Books Ltd in 2016 and distributed by

Parragon Inc.
440 Park Avenue South, 13th Floor
New York, NY 10016
www.parragon.com/lovefood

LOVE FOOD is an imprint of Parragon Books Ltd

ISBN 978-1-4748-1773-8

Printed in China

New cover photography by Tony Briscoe
New recipes, introduction, and incidental text by Robin Donovan
New photography by Ian Garlick
Edited by Fiona Biggs

Notes for the Reader
This book uses standard kitchen measuring spoons and cups. All spoon and cup measurements are level unless otherwise indicated. Unless otherwise stated, milk is assumed to be whole, eggs are large, individual fruits and vegetables are medium, pepper is freshly ground black pepper, and salt is table salt. A pinch of salt is calculated as $\frac{1}{16}$ of a teaspoon. Unless otherwise stated, all root vegetables should be peeled prior to using.

The times given are an approximate guide only. Preparation times differ according to the techniques used by different people, and the cooking times may also vary from those given.

Please note that any ingredients stated as being optional are not included in the nutritional values provided. The nutritional values given are approximate and provided as a guideline only; they do not account for individual cooks, scales, and portion sizes. The nutritional values provided are per serving or per item.

CONTENTS

INTRODUCTION 6

INTRODUCTION

What is a nut? Botanically speaking, a nut is a hard-shelled pod that contains a single seed and doesn't open when the fruit is mature. These include chestnuts, hazelnuts, and acorns. However, in the culinary world, the word "nut" has a much broader definition, including: certain drupes (a fruit with flesh surrounding a shell or a pit with a single seed inside), such as walnuts, almonds, pecans, macadamia nuts, and coconuts; some legumes, which grow in multi-seeded pods that split open to reveal the seeds, such as peanuts; and various other seeds, such as pine nuts, cashew nuts, and Brazil nuts. For our purposes, these are all nuts.

Nuts in all their variety may just be the most underrated heroes of the food world. There's no denying that these little morsels are delicious—whether eaten on their own or tossed into salads, stirred into cookie dough, baked into muffins or cakes, or sprinkled over ice cream, yogurt, or oatmeal. Part of their allure is their versatility: they can be eaten raw or toasted, whole or chopped, or ground into flours or butters. What's more, you can carry them with you wherever you go, and they have a long shelf life.

Adding to their superpowers, nuts are also absolutely packed with nutrition. They are full of the protein, fiber, vitamins, minerals, and healthy fats that help you curb your appetite, protect against heart disease, lower cholesterol, and reduce your risk of developing cancer.

If you're a vegetarian or vegan, nuts can be an especially important part of your healthy diet because they are a great source of protein and one of the best plant-based sources of healthy fats. Nut butters, particularly, are a great way to get quick protein when you don't eat meat.

In short, nuts—ranging from almonds, walnuts, and hazelnuts to cashews, Brazil nuts, and pistachios—are great for your health and your palate, so what are you waiting for? Experiment with some of the recipes shown here and both your taste buds and your body will thank you.

BRAZIL NUT

MACADAMIA NUT

CASHEW NUT

HAZELNUT

CHESTNUT

ALMOND

PINE NUT

WALNUT

PECAN

PEANUT

PISTACHIO

SPREADS & SNACKS

Maple & Cinnamon Cashew Nut Butter	12
Vanilla & Macadamia Nut Butter	14
Roasted Almond Gingersnap Butter	16
Pumpkin Pecan Butter	18
Cayenne Pepper & Lime Peanut Butter	20
Homemade Cacao & Hazelnut Butter	22
NUT BUTTERS	24
Five-Spice Cashew Nuts	26
Chewy Apricot & Almond Energy Bars	28
Walnut & Flaxseed Crackers	30
Chocolate & Peanut Butter Energy Balls	32
Pecan Oat Cakes	34
Raw Date & Coconut Bars	36
Mixed Nuts in Herbed Salt	38

MAPLE & CINNAMON CASHEW NUT BUTTER

Really creamy, just a little sweet, and with a kick of cinnamon, this rich nut butter is simply delicious spread on toast or apple wedges, as a sandwich filling, or for any little treat where you'd normally enjoy a dollop of peanut butter.

MAKES: 1½ cups   **PREP TIME:** 5 mins   **COOK TIME:** none

INGREDIENTS

2 cups unsalted roasted cashew nuts

3 tablespoons maple syrup

1 teaspoon vanilla extract

¾ teaspoon cinnamon

pinch of salt

2 teaspoons coconut oil

1. Put the nuts into a food processor and process for 1 minute. Scrape down the side of the bowl and process the contents again for 1–2 minutes. Repeat until you have a smooth paste.

2. Add the maple syrup, vanilla extract, cinnamon, and salt and continue processing until the mixture is smooth. With the processor running, add the oil and process until well combined.

3. Serve immediately or store in a covered container in the refrigerator for several weeks.

per 1½ cups: 1685 cals / 124.9g fat / 30.7g sat fat / 124g carbs / 49.4g sugars / 8.5g protein / 38.4g fiber / 640g sodium

VANILLA & MACADAMIA NUT BUTTER

Macadamia nuts are rich in flavor and have a distinctively creamy texture. Because of their high oil content, they become runny when ground. Cashew nuts, which are milder in flavor but sturdier in consistency when ground, provide good structure to this butter, making it especially spreadable.

MAKES: 1½ cups   **PREP TIME:** 5 mins   **COOK TIME:** none

INGREDIENTS

1 cup roasted, unsalted macadamia nuts

1 cup roasted, unsalted cashew nuts

1 teaspoon vanilla extract

¼ teaspoon salt

1. Put the macadamia nuts and cashew nuts into a food processor and process for 3–4 minutes, until smooth.

2. Add the vanilla extract and salt and process to incorporate. Serve immediately or transfer to a covered container and store in the refrigerator for up to 3 weeks.

per 1½ cups: 1,670 cals / 158.3g fat / 27.1g sat fat / 57.8g carbs / 12.1g sugars / 14.4g fiber / 28.9g protein / 600g sodium

ROASTED ALMOND GINGERSNAP BUTTER

Lightly sweetened with molasses and brown sugar and spiced with both fresh and ground ginger, this healthy nut butter tastes just like gingersnaps. Try it spread on crisp apples as a light snack, or have it on toast with sliced pears.

MAKES: 1½ cups   **PREP TIME:** 10 mins   **COOK TIME:** none

INGREDIENTS

2 cups roasted almonds

2 tablespoons packed light brown sugar

2 tablespoons molasses

1½ teaspoons grated fresh ginger

½ teaspoon ground ginger

¼ teaspoon salt

2–3 tablespoons grapeseed oil

1. Put the almonds into a food processor and process for 5–10 minutes, until smooth.

2. Add the sugar, molasses, fresh ginger, ground ginger, and salt and process until well combined. With the processor running, add the oil, a little at a time, until you achieve the desired consistency.

3. Serve immediately or refrigerate until ready to use. Almond butter can be stored in the refrigerator for several weeks.

> **TIP:** *It can take a while for almonds to release their oils so that your almond butter has the consistency you're after. Don't give up. Keep processing (giving your food processor a break now and then if it begins to overheat) until you get a smooth, creamy paste, which could take as long as 10 minutes or more.*

per 12 oz: 2,204 cals / 182.3g fat / 14.8g sat fat / 110.5g carbs / 63g sugars / 31.2g fiber / 60.5g protein / 600g sodium

PUMPKIN PECAN BUTTER

This tasty butter offers everything you love about pumpkin pie filling but in a spread that's perfect on toast, muffins, or fruit.

MAKES: about 2 cups   **PREP TIME:** 5 mins, plus cooling   **COOK TIME:** 8–10 mins

INGREDIENTS

½ cup chopped pecans

⅓ cup packed firmly light brown sugar

1 (15-ounce) can pumpkin puree

1 tablespoon molasses

½ teaspoon ground cinnamon

½ teaspoon ground allspice

⅛ teaspoon ground cloves

⅛ teaspoon ground nutmeg

¼ teaspoon salt

1. Put the nuts into a food processor and process for 2–3 minutes, until smooth. Scrape the mixture into a medium saucepan.

2. Add the remaining ingredients and bring to a boil over medium–high heat. Reduce the heat to low and cook for 8–10 minutes, stirring frequently, until the mixture darkens and becomes thick.

3. Let cool to room temperature. Serve immediately or store in a covered container in the refrigerator for up to 1 week.

per 2 cups:: 923 cals / 41g fat / 4.1g sat fat / 142.9g carbs / 115.3g sugars / 18.7g fiber / 10g protein / 640g sodium

CAYENNE PEPPER & LIME PEANUT BUTTER

This sweet-and -spicy peanut butter will change the way you think of the humble peanut-butter sandwich forever. Try it spread between slices of toasted whole-wheat bread with a slice of ripe tomato, crunchy cucumber, and a crisp lettuce leaf.

MAKES: 1½ cups   **PREP TIME:** 5 mins   **COOK TIME:** none

INGREDIENTS

1½ cups roasted, unsalted peanuts

½ teaspoon cayenne pepper

¼ teaspoon salt

grated zest and juice of 1 lime

1 teaspoon packed light brown sugar

1 tablespoon coconut oil

1. Put the peanuts into a food processor and process for 2–3 minutes, until smooth. Add the cayenne pepper, salt, lime zest and juice, and sugar and process until well combined.

2. With the machine running, add the oil and process until the mixture is smooth and well incorporated. Serve immediately or transfer to a jar and store in the refrigerator for several weeks.

> **TIP:** *This peanut butter makes a great sauce for pasta or noodles. Toss a few tablespoons of the butter, along with a splash of the noodle cooking water, with hot spaghetti or rice noodles. Add shredded cooked chicken or diced tofu to make it a meal, and garnish with chopped fresh cilantro and sliced scallions.*

per 1½ cups: 1,510 cals / 125.5g fat / 27.3g sat fat / 68g carbs / 25.1g sugars / 18.8g fiber / 53.7g protein / 600g sodium

HOMEMADE CACAO & HAZELNUT BUTTER

This delicious nut butter, made with wholesome ingredients, is perfect spread on whole-grain toast or hot pancakes for a weekend treat.

MAKES: ¾ cup   **PREP TIME:** 15 mins, plus standing   **COOK TIME:** 3–4 mins

INGREDIENTS

1 cup unblanched hazelnuts

¼ cup raw cacao powder

⅓ cup firmly packed light brown sugar

½ cup light olive oil

½ teaspoon vanilla extract

pinch of sea salt

1. Add the hazelnuts to a dry skillet and cook over medium heat for 3–4 minutes, constantly shaking the pan, until the nuts are an even golden brown.

2. Wrap the nuts in a clean dish towel and rub to remove the skins.

3. Put the nuts into a blender and blend until finely ground. Add the cacao powder, sugar, oil, vanilla extract, and salt and blend again until smooth.

4. Spoon into a small jar with an airtight lid and seal. Let stand at room temperature for 4 hours, until the sugar has dissolved completely. Stir again, then store in the refrigerator for up to 5 days.

per ¾ cup: 430 cals / 40g fat / 5.2g sat fat / 19.5g carbs / 13.9g sugars / 4g fiber / 4.1g protein / 120g sodium

1

2

3

NUT BUTTERS

You can buy a jar of peanut butter or almond butter in any supermarket, but in just a few minutes and at a fraction of the cost, you can make your own delicious—and far more exotic—nut butters right in your own kitchen. Once you get the hang of making a basic nut butter, you'll be free to concoct the flavor combinations of your dreams.

The flavor combinations possible for homemade nut butters are endless and intoxicating: macadamia and roasted almond; hazelnut and chocolate; cashew and cinnamon; maple and pecan—the list goes on.

Making nut butters couldn't be simpler. The only tool you need is a good food processor or a high-speed blender. A handful of nuts and whatever add-ins you'd like—honey, maple syrup, cocoa powder, ground cinnamon, or other spices, raisins, golden raisins, or other dried fruits, chocolate chips: you name it—will quickly be transformed into a delectable nut butter.

These delightful spreads can dress up a plain piece of toast, but they also make a fantastic dip for fresh fruit, a great filling for sandwiches, or a delicious spread for cookies. You could add some to a cookie dough or cake batter for extra flavor, or swirl it into brownie or muffin batter just before baking. A savory nut butter also makes a delicious sauce when tossed with hot noodles or pasta or drizzled over cooked vegetables.

HERE'S HOW:

1. Place the nuts in your food processor or blender.

2. Pulse several times to grind the nuts. If you prefer a chunky nut butter, remove a small portion of the nuts now and reserve them to add back in later.

3. Process for 1 minute, scrape down the side and bottom of the bowl, and process again for 1 minute. Repeat until the mixture is smooth and creamy.

4. Add salt, oil, sweeteners, or other flavorings. Process for an additional 2–3 minutes, until the mixture is smooth. If you've reserved some coarsely chopped nuts, or if you're using other ingredients, such as chocolate chips, add them now and pulse to incorporate.

5. Enjoy!

TOP 5 TIPS FOR MAKING HOMEMADE NUT BUTTERS

1. Use a powerful food processor or high-speed blender.

2. For the best flavor and texture, you should toast your nuts just before processing them.

3. Be patient. It takes a while, but if you process your nuts for long enough, you'll experience a magical moment when they transform into a creamy and utterly divine spread.

4. For added creaminess and cohesiveness, add a little oil—peanut, coconut, or grapeseed oils are ideal.

5. Be creative. Use a combination of nuts and add different sweeteners, spices, extracts, or other ingredients. The possibilities are endless.

FIVE-SPICE CASHEW NUTS

Peppercorns, star anise, fennel, cloves, and cinnamon combine here with the natural sweetness of cashews. For a moreish snack or a pre-dinner or barbecue appetizer with a spicy character, this nutty concoction performs at every level.

SERVES: 8   **PREP TIME:** 5 mins   **COOK TIME:** 10–12 mins

INGREDIENTS

1 tablespoon peanut oil, for oiling

½ teaspoon Sichuan peppercorns

2 star anise pods

½ teaspoon fennel seeds

6 whole cloves

½ teaspoon ground cinnamon

2 tablespoons water

¼ cup firmly packed light brown sugar

1 teaspoon salt

2 cups toasted unsalted cashew nuts

1. Preheat the oven to 400°F. Lightly oil a baking sheet and a large piece of aluminum foil.

2. In a spice grinder, grind together the peppercorns, star anise pods, fennel seeds, and cloves until finely ground. Add the cinnamon and mix well.

3. Put the water and sugar into a medium saucepan and heat over medium heat, stirring constantly, for 2 minutes, or until the sugar is dissolved. Add the spice mixture and salt and stir to mix well. Add the nuts and stir to coat completely. Cook, stirring, for an additional minute.

4. Transfer the nuts to the prepared pan and spread out in an even layer. Roast in the preheated oven for 6–8 minutes, until most of the liquid has evaporated. Transfer the nuts to the prepared foil and separate them so that they don't stick together. Let cool completely before serving.

5. Store in an airtight container at room temperature for up to 2 weeks.

per serving: 219 cals / 16.2g fat / 3.2g sat fat / 16.6g carbs / 7.6g sugars / 1.1g fiber / 4.8g protein / 720g sodium

CHEWY APRICOT & ALMOND ENERGY BARS

*These oat-bar-style, dairy-free energy bars are great for carrying
with you for a healthy midmorning snack.*

MAKES: 15   **PREP TIME:** 25 mins, plus cooling   **COOK TIME:** 30 mins

INGREDIENTS

½ cup coconut oil

⅓ cup firmly packed
light brown sugar

¼ cup almond butter

1 crisp sweet apple,
such as Pippin, cored
and coarsely grated

2 cups rolled oats

¼ cup brown rice flour

¼ cup coarsely chopped
unblanched almonds

¼ cup sunflower seeds

1½ cups diced dried
apricots

1. Preheat the oven to 350°F. Line an 8-inch shallow square cake pan with nonstick parchment paper.

2. Heat the oil and sugar in a medium saucepan over low heat until the oil has melted and the sugar has dissolved. Remove from the heat and add the almond butter, stirring until melted.

3. Add the apple, oats, flour, almonds, and sunflower seeds and mix well together.

4. Spoon two-thirds of the dough into the prepared pan and press down firmly. Sprinkle with the apricots and firmly press into the bottom layer, then dot the remaining oat mixture over the top in a thin layer so that some of the apricots are still visible.

5. Bake in the preheated oven for about 25 minutes, until the top is golden brown. Remove from the oven and let cool in the pan until almost cold, then cut into 15 small rectangles. Let cool completely, then lift the bars out of the pan, using the paper. Separate the bars and pack into a plastic container. Store in the refrigerator for up to 3 days.

per bar: 235 cals / 14g fat / 7.2g sat fat / 26.6g carbs / 14.6g sugars / 3.5g fiber / 4.2g protein/ trace sodium

WALNUT & FLAXSEED CRACKERS

Walnuts and flaxseed combine in a cracker to create a nutritional powerhouse. Walnuts, one of the most health-giving nuts, include omega-3 fats, amino acids, and antioxidants, and flaxseed is a rich source of micronutrients, manganese, and vitamin B1.

MAKES: 40   **PREP TIME:** 20 mins, plus chilling   **COOK TIME:** 22 mins

INGREDIENTS

⅔ cup ground flaxseed

1¼ cups whole-wheat flour, plus 1 tablespoon for dusting

½ teaspoon salt

2 tablespoons packed light brown sugar

6 tablespoons unsalted butter, at room temperature

½ cup milk

1 cup raisins

½ cup chopped walnuts

3 tablespoons whole flaxseed

1. Preheat the oven to 350°F. Put the ground flaxseed, flour, salt, and sugar into a large mixing bowl and mix with a handheld electric mixer. Add the butter and mix on medium speed for 2–3 minutes, until coarse crumbs form.

2. Add the milk, raisins, walnuts, and whole flaxseed and mix until the dough comes together. Turn out the dough onto a piece of plastic wrap and shape it into a disk. Wrap in the plastic wrap and chill in the refrigerator for about 10 minutes.

3. Lay a large sheet of parchment paper on a work surface. Turn out the dough onto the paper and flatten it into a large rectangle with the palms of your hands. Sprinkle with a little flour, then roll out as thinly as possible (to the thickness of the chopped nuts).

4. Using a sharp knife, score the dough into 2-inch squares. Slide the paper onto a large baking sheet and bake in the preheated oven for 20–22 minutes, until the crackers are lightly browned. Remove from the oven, break the crackers apart, and let cool before serving.

per cracker: 68 cals / 4g fat / 1.4g sat fat / 7.6g carbs / 3.1g sugars / 1.4g fiber / 1.5g protein / 40g sodium

1

2

3

CHOCOLATE & PEANUT BUTTER ENERGY BALLS

Nuts and chocolate are an almost irresistible combination. These delicious little balls will give you an energy boost at any time of day.

MAKES: 8   **PREP TIME:** 15 mins, plus chilling   **COOK TIME:** none

INGREDIENTS

⅓ cup blanched almonds

¼ cup unsweetened peanut butter

2 tablespoons coarsely chopped unsalted peanuts

3 tablespoons flaxseed

1 ounce bittersweet chocolate, finely chopped

pinch of salt

1 teaspoon unsweetened cocoa powder

1. Put the almonds into a food processor and process for 1 minute, until you have almond meal.

2. Put the peanut butter, peanuts, flaxseed, chocolate, and salt into a bowl and mix to combine. Add the almond meal, reserving 1½ tablespoons. Mix until the texture resembles chunky clay.

3. Sprinkle the remaining almond meal and the cocoa powder onto a plate and mix with a teaspoon. Shape a tablespoon-size blob of the peanut mixture into a ball, using your palms. Roll it in the cocoa powder mixture, then transfer to a clean plate. Make an additional seven balls in the same way.

4. Cover and chill in the refrigerator for at least 30 minutes or up to 2 days before serving.

> **TIP:** *If the coating of cocoa powder is too bitter and strong for your taste, substitute it with a teaspoon of ground cinnamon.*

per ball: 144 cals / 11.9g fat / 2.1g sat fat / 5.9g carbs / 1.7g sugars / 3.0g fiber / 4.9g protein / 120g sodium

PECAN OAT CAKES

These Scottish-style oat cakes are studded with crunchy chopped pecans, giving them a nutty flavor and added texture. They make the perfect accompaniment to a cheese plate, or you could eat them on their own as a simple snack.

MAKES: 40   **PREP TIME:** 20 mins, plus cooling   **COOK TIME:** 15 mins

INGREDIENTS

1 cup rolled oats

1 cup all-purpose flour, plus 1 tablespoons for dusting

¾ teaspoon sugar

½ teaspoon baking soda

¼ teaspoon salt

1 stick chilled unsalted butter, cut into small pieces

3 tablespoons water

½ cup chopped pecans

1. Preheat the oven to 375°F.

2. Put the oats, flour, sugar, baking soda, and salt into a food processor. Add the butter and pulse until the mixture resembles coarse crumbs. With the processor running, slowly add the water and process until the mixture comes together in a thick dough. Add the nuts and pulse until they are just incorporated.

3. Turn out the dough onto a sheet of parchment paper and lightly dust with flour. Using a lightly floured rolling pin, roll out the dough to a thin rectangle. Score the dough into 2-inch squares with a sharp knife.

4. Transfer the squares on the parchment paper to a baking sheet and bake in the preheated oven for 13–15 minutes, until light brown and crisp. Remove from the oven and transfer on the paper to a wire rack. Let cool completely before removing from the paper. Serve at room temperature.

per oatcake: 53 cals / 3.4g fat / 1.6g sat fat / 4.3g carbs / 0.2g sugars / 0.4g fiber / 0.8g protein / 40g sodium

RAW DATE & COCONUT BARS

*These chunky, nutty bars get the most out of power-packed raw ingredients.
They are the perfect way of keeping you energized throughout the afternoon.*

MAKES: 12   PREP TIME: 30 mins , plus chilling   COOK TIME: none

INGREDIENTS

16 medjool dates,
halved and pitted

⅓ cup unblanched almonds

½ cup cashew nut pieces

2 tablespoons chia seeds

2 tablespoons maca
(powdered superfood)

2 teaspoons vanilla extract

¼ cup flaked unsweetened
dried coconut

½ cup coarsely chopped
unblanched hazelnuts

¼ cup pecan halves

1. Put the dates, almonds, and cashew pieces into a food processor and process until finely chopped.

2. Add the chia seeds, maca, and vanilla extract and process again until the mixture binds together in a coarse ball.

3. Tear off two sheets of nonstick parchment paper, put one on the work surface, and sprinkle with half the coconut. Put the date ball on top, then press into a coarse rectangle with your fingertips. Cover with the second sheet of paper and roll out to a 12 x 8-inch rectangle. Lift off the top piece of paper, sprinkle with the remaining coconut, the hazelnuts, and pecans, then cover again with the paper and briefly roll with a rolling pin to press the nuts into the date mixture.

4. Loosen the top paper, then transfer the date mixture, still on the bottom paper, to a tray and chill for 3 hours or overnight, until firm.

5. Remove the top paper, cut the date mixture into 12 pieces, peel off the bottom paper, then pack the bars into a plastic container, layering with pieces of parchment paper to keep them separate. Store in the refrigerator for up to 3 days.

per bar: 225 cals / 11g fat / 2g sat fat / 31.7g carbs / 23.5g sugars / 5.4g fiber / 4.2g protein / trace sodium

MIXED NUTS
IN HERBED SALT

*Simple to make and wonderfully tasty, these addictive pan-roasted nuts
are bursting with protein, healthy fats, and plenty of flavor.*

SERVES: 4   **PREP TIME:** 5 mins, plus cooling   **COOK TIME:** 5 mins

INGREDIENTS

1 tablespoon olive oil

2 fresh rosemary sprigs,
leaves torn from the stems

½ cup cashew nuts

½ cup pecans

½ cup unblanched almonds

⅓ cup unblanched hazelnuts

½ teaspoon sea salt

1. Heat the oil and rosemary in a medium skillet, then swirl the oil around the pan to pick up flavor from the rosemary. Add the nuts and cook over medium heat for 2–3 minutes, until lightly toasted.

2. Stir in the salt, then spoon the nuts into a bowl and let cool before eating. Any leftover nuts can be stored in the refrigerator in a plastic container or airtight jar for up to 3 days.

TIP: *Try replacing the rosemary with a little curry powder or a blend of ground turmeric, garam masala, smoked paprika, and a pinch of chili powder.*

per serving: 366 cals / 34.4g fat / 3.5g sat fat / 11.3g carbs / 2.5g sugars / 4.8g fiber / 8.7g protein / 280g sodium

BREAKFAST & BRUNCH

VANILLA, ALMOND & BANANA SMOOTHIE

This almond-based smoothie is sweetened only with dates, but it tastes as sweet and delicious as the best milk shake you ever had – it is also packed with protein!

SERVES: 2   **PREP TIME:** 5 mins   **COOK TIME:** 5 mins

INGREDIENTS

1 cup almond milk

¼ cup almond butter

1 banana

4 pitted dates

1 teaspoon vanilla extract

8–10 ice cubes

1. Put all of the ingredients into a blender and blend on high speed until smooth.

2. Pour into two glasses and serve immediately.

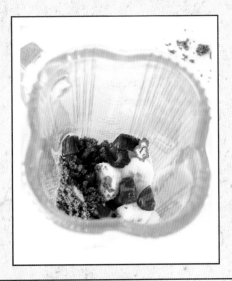

TIP: *When buying almond milk, choose one made with just almonds and water, if possible—some varieties have added sugar. Freeze almond milk as you would cow milk; it will separate, so when it has thawed, blend it for a few seconds before serving.*

per serving: 330 cals / 18.1g fat / 1.4g sat fat / 31.4g carbs / 24.4g sugars / 6.4g fibre / 9.4g protein / 80g sodium

PROTEIN BERRY WHIP

Frozen berries are a healthy and handy freezer staple. Process with protein-boosting cashew nuts and Brazil nuts for a delicious shake.

SERVES: 4   PREP TIME: 10–15 mins   COOK TIME: none

INGREDIENTS

¾ cup frozen sliced strawberries

¾ cup frozen blueberries

12 Brazil nuts

⅓ cup cashew nut pieces

⅓ cup rolled oats

2 cups almond milk

2 tablespoons maple syrup

1. Put the strawberries, blueberries, Brazil nuts, and cashew nut pieces into a blender. Add the oats, then pour in half the almond milk. Blend until smooth.

2. Add the remaining milk and the maple syrup, then blend again until smooth. Pour into four glasses and serve immediately with spoons. As the drink stands, the blueberries will almost set the liquid, but as soon as you stir it, it will turn to liquid again.

per serving: 213 cals / 12.8g fat / 2.4g sat fat / 23.2g carbs / 11.6g sugars / 3.5g fibre / 4.7g protein / 80g sodium

1

2

3

PEANUT BUTTER & BANANA PANCAKES

Peanut butter and banana is a time-honored combination for good reason. Here, the dynamic duo flavors fluffy pancakes finished off with a rich and decadent peanut-butter-flavored maple syrup.

SERVES: 4   **PREP TIME:** 20 mins, plus standing   **COOK TIME:** 15 mins

INGREDIENTS

1 cup roasted, unsalted peanuts

¾ cup whole-wheat flour

¾ cup all-purpose flour

2 tablespoons packed light brown sugar

2 teaspoons baking powder

pinch of salt

2 ripe bananas

1½ cups milk

2 eggs

2 tablespoons butter

¾ cup maple syrup

1. Put the peanuts into a food processor and process for 2–3 minutes, until smooth.

2. Put the whole-wheat flour, all-purpose flour, sugar, baking powder, and salt into a medium mixing bowl. Put 1 banana into a separate large mixing bowl, mash well, then add the milk, eggs, and half the peanut butter and stir until well combined. Add the dry mixture to the wet mixture and mix with a handheld electric mixer until well combined, adding a little more milk, if needed. Let stand for 5 minutes.

3. Thinly slice the remaining banana.

4. Heat 1 tablespoon of the butter in a large skillet over medium–high heat. Add the batter, ⅓ cup per pancake (cooking in batches), and top each pancake with 3–5 banana slices, pressing them into the batter. Cook for 2–3 minutes, until bubbles form and begin to burst on top of the pancakes. Flip the pancakes over and cook for an additional 1–2 minutes, until golden brown. Repeat with the remaining batter, adding additional butter to the pan as needed.

5. Meanwhile, combine the maple syrup and the remaining peanut butter in a small saucepan and heat over medium heat, stirring frequently, until hot and well combined. Keep warm until ready to serve.

6. Serve the pancakes hot, drizzled with the syrup.

per serving: 700 cals / 29.3g fat / 8.6g sat fat / 96.1g carbs / 47.2g sugars / 7.3g fibre / 20.2g protein / 530g sodium

VANILLA & BERRY OVERNIGHT OATMEAL

Oatmeal for breakfast doesn't get any easier than this. Combine oats and milk (any type) before you go to bed and when you wake up in the morning, breakfast is ready. There are endless possible variations on this simple and satisfying breakfast.

SERVES: 2   **PREP TIME:** 5 mins, plus chilling   **COOK TIME:** none

INGREDIENTS

⅔ cup rolled oats

⅔ cup unsweetened almond milk

½ teaspoon vanilla extract

2 teaspoons honey

¼ cup vanilla yogurt

¼ cup blueberries

¼ cup sliced strawberries

1 tablespoon toasted sliced almonds

1. Put the oats into a serving bowl. Pour the almond milk over the oats and add the vanilla extract and honey. Stir, cover and refrigerate for at least 4 hours or overnight.

2. Remove the mixture from the refrigerator, add the yogurt, and stir well. Top with the blueberries, strawberries, and almonds and serve immediately.

TIP: *Substitute any type of milk—cow, coconut, cashew nut, rice, soy, etc. Or vary the flavor with different fresh or dried fruits, nuts, or by adding natural sweeteners, such as maple syrup or agave nectar.*

per serving: 199 cals / 5.5g fat / 0.8g sat fat / 31.9g carbs / 13.2g sugars / 4g fibre / 6.2g protein / 40g sodium

YOGURT WITH BLUEBERRIES, HONEY & NUTS

Greek yogurt topped with fresh berries, honey, and nuts is quick to make and is a delicious breakfast treat.

SERVES: 4   **PREP TIME:** 10 mins, plus chilling   **COOK TIME:** 5 mins

INGREDIENTS

3 tablespoons honey

⅓ cup unsalted cashew nuts

⅓ cup hazelnuts

½ cup Greek-style plain yogurt

1⅓ cups blueberries

1. Heat the honey in a small saucepan over medium heat.

2. Stir in the nuts until well coated. Remove from the heat and let cool slightly.

3. Spoon the yogurt into four bowls, then spoon the nuts and blueberries over it. Serve immediately.

per serving: 225 cals / 11.9g fat / 1.8g sat fat / 27.7g carbs / 21g sugars / 3.1g fibre / 5.8g protein / trace sodium

SPICED QUINOA BREAKFAST BOWL WITH PECANS

Quinoa is packed with protein, making it a fantastic grain to include in a healthy breakfast. Here, it's combined with zingy spices, sweet pears, and crunchy nuts for a breakfast that's worth getting out of bed for.

SERVES: 2   **PREP TIME:** 15 mins   **COOK TIME:** 15 mins

INGREDIENTS

⅓ cup uncooked quinoa, rinsed well

⅔ cup water

¼ teaspoon ground cinnamon

pinch of nutmeg

pinch of allspice

pinch of salt

4 teaspoons maple syrup

½ cup almond milk

1 pear, cored and diced

⅓ cup pecans, toasted

1. In a small saucepan, combine the quinoa with the water, cinnamon, nutmeg, allspice, and salt and bring to a boil over medium–high heat. Reduce the heat to low, cover, and simmer for about 15 minutes, until the quinoa is tender.

2. Stir in the maple syrup and divide the mixture between two serving bowls. Pour the almond milk over the top, dividing it equally, and garnish with the pear pieces and pecans. Serve immediately.

per serving: 320 cals / 15.5g fat / 1.4g sat fat / 42.9g carbs / 17.3g sugars / 6.8g fibre / 6.1g protein / 320g soldium

HEALTH-GIVING NUTS

The reputed ability of nuts to reduce the risk of developing cancer is the attribute that really solidifies their designation as a superfood, but they also have other nutrients that give them an enviable reputation as a health powerhouse. Unsaturated fats (also referred to as "good fats")—both monounsaturated and polyunsaturated—can help lower bad cholesterol levels, while omega-3 fatty acids help protect you from heart attacks. Incorporating nuts into your daily diet is an easy—and tasty—way to boost your health.

ALMONDS

High in vitamin E, the B vitamins, and magnesium, which help to shore up your immune system. They also contain more fiber than any other nut, which can help you curb your appetite and control your blood sugar.

CASHEW NUTS

Contain loads of iron and zinc, which help carry oxygen to your cells, prevent anemia, boost your immune system, and support healthy vision. With the added bonus of a high dose of magnesium, a daily serving of these nuts could help improve your memory and protect against age-related memory loss.

BRAZIL NUTS

High in selenium, a mineral that may protect against bone, prostate, and breast cancers.

CHESTNUTS

Have a generous quantity of the B vitamins that help produce red blood cells; break down protein, carbs, and fats for energy; give you healthy skin; and boost brain function.

HAZELNUTS

Hazelnuts are rich in vitamin E, which can help prevent cataracts and macular degeneration, maintain healthy skin, and reduce the risk of dementia.

MACADAMIA NUTS

Calorie-dense, but they also deliver the highest levels of heart-healthy monounsaturated fats, which help to lower cholesterol and blood pressure.

PEANUTS

A great source of copper, an essential mineral for red blood cell formation and for building a healthy immune system, blood vessels, and bones.

PECANS

Loaded with antioxidants, which help prevent dangerous plaque buildup in your arteries.

PINE NUTS

Contain high levels of vitamins A and lutein, which support healthy vision. Their high vitamin D content helps to build strong bones and teeth.

PISTACHIO NUTS

High in gamma-tocopherol, a type of vitamin E that may play a role in reducing lung cancer risk. Loaded with potassium and vitamin B6, they can also help keep your nervous system and muscles healthy, boost your mood, and bolster your immune system.

WALNUTS

Beat all other nuts for high levels of antioxidants, which protect your body from the type of cellular damage that can lead to heart disease, cancer, and premature aging. They're also an aid to reducing the high levels of stress that can lead to illness and a depressed immune system.

SWEET POTATO PANCAKES & CINNAMON CASHEW CREAM

Shredded sweet potato pancakes topped with a lightly sweetened cashew cream make a nutritious and satisfying breakfast or brunch.

SERVES: 4   PREP TIME: 15 mins, plus soaking   COOK TIME: 40 mins

INGREDIENTS

CASHEW CREAM

1 cup unsalted cashew nuts, soaked in water overnight, drained, and rinsed

½ cup water

2 tablespoons maple syrup

½ teaspoon cinnamon

pinch of salt

PANCAKES

2 sweet potatoes, peeled and shredded

2 tablespoons flour

pinch of salt

2 extra-large eggs, lightly beaten

2 tablespoons sunflower oil, for frying

1. To make the cashew cream, put the nuts into a blender with the water. Blend on medium speed, scraping down the side of the blender as needed, for 3–5 minutes, until the nuts are pureed to a smooth consistency. Add the maple syrup, cinnamon, and salt and process on high speed until the mixture is smooth and well combined.

2. To make the pancakes, combine the sweet potatoes, flour, and salt in a large mixing bowl, tossing to mix well. Add the eggs and mix well.

3. Heat 1 tablespoon of the oil in a large skillet over medium–high heat. Scoop the sweet potato batter into the pan, using ½ cup of batter for each pancake. Flatten the pancakes slightly with the back of the spoon as you put them in the pan. Cover and cook for about 5 minutes, until the pancakes are brown underneath. Flip over and cook, covered, for an additional 5 minutes to brown the other side.

4. Repeat with the remaining batter, adding more oil as needed. Serve hot, with a drizzle of the cashew cream.

per serving: 401 cals / 24.1g fat / 4.2g sat fat / 37.5g carbs / 11.7g sugars / 4g fibre / 11.6g protein / 400g sodium

1

2

3

CARROT CAKE MUFFINS

These sweet treats pack a healthy enough punch to make them a perfectly reasonable breakfast option. Full of nutrient-rich carrots, raisins, and walnuts, and sweetened with a combination of brown sugar and applesauce, they're sure to make you happy at any time of the day.

MAKES: 12   **PREP TIME:** 15 mins, plus cooling   **COOK TIME:** 22 mins

INGREDIENTS

½ tablespoon butter, for greasing

¾ cup whole-wheat flour

½ cup all-purpose flour

1 teaspoon baking soda

1½ teaspoons cinnamon

½ teaspoon ground ginger

½ teaspoon salt

⅔ cup firmly packed light brown sugar

½ cup unsweetened applesauce

¼ cup sunflower oil

1 teaspoon vanilla extract

2 eggs, at room temperature

2 carrots, finely grated

¼ cup raisins

¼ cup chopped walnuts

1. Preheat the oven to 350°F and grease a 12-cup muffin pan.

2. Put the whole-wheat flour, all-purpose flour, baking soda, cinnamon, ginger, and salt into a medium bowl and mix to combine.

3. Put the sugar, applesauce, and oil into a separate bowl and beat with a handheld electric mixer until well combined. Add the vanilla extract and then add the eggs, one at a time, beating well after each addition.

4. Add the dry mixture to the wet mixture and beat for 1 minute, until just combined. Gently stir in the carrots, raisins, and walnuts. Scoop the batter into the prepared pan.

5. Bake in the preheated oven for 20–22 minutes, or until a toothpick inserted into the center of a muffin comes out clean. Let cool in the pan for a few minutes, then transfer the muffins to a wire rack and let cool completely. Serve warm or at room temperature.

per muffin: 187 cals / 7.6g fat / 1.3g sat fat / 27.8g carbs / 16.7g sugars / 1.8g fibre / 3.1g protein / 240g sodium

COFFEE & PECAN MINI BREAKFAST MUFFINS

Sometimes you feel you need a sweet hit in the morning to get you through the first few hours. These little muffins provide that with none of the sugar highs and crashes.

MAKES: 9   **PREP TIME:** 25 mins, plus cooling   **COOK TIME:** 20 mins

INGREDIENTS

½ cup coconut flour

¼ teaspoon baking powder

½ teaspoon baking soda

1 tablespoon stevia

¼ cup coarsely chopped pecans

pinch of sea salt

⅔ cup sour cream

⅓ cup vegetable oil

2 extra-large eggs, beaten

⅓ cup prepared espresso coffee

1 teaspoon rice malt syrup

1. Preheat the oven to 325°F. Put nine paper mini muffin liners into a mini muffin pan.

2. Put the flour, baking powder, baking soda, stevia, 3 tablespoons of the pecans, and the salt into a large bowl and mix well. Add the sour cream, oil, eggs, and ¼ cup of the coffee, and stir until evenly mixed. Let stand for a moment, then spoon the batter into the mini muffin liners.

3. Bake in the preheated oven for 20 minutes, or until well risen and the tops spring back when pressed with a fingertip. Let cool in the pan for 5 minutes, then transfer to a wire rack.

4. To make the topping, put the rice malt syrup and remaining coffee into a bowl and mix. Spoon a small drizzle over each muffin. Sprinkle with the remaining pecans and serve warm, or store in an airtight container for up to 2 days.

TIP: *Baking with rice malt syrup is similar to baking with sugar in terms of quantity and texture. However, be aware that it can burn quickly. You can prevent this by loosely placing a sheet of baking paper over the top of your pan to protect the exposed areas while allowing the rest to bake.*

per muffin: 170 cals / 16.6g fat / 3.2g sat fat / 1.6g carbs / 1.1g sugars / 0.5g fibre / 3.6g protein / 200g sodium

CHIA SEED & PISTACHIO BREAKFAST PUDDING

Overnight soaking in creamy almond milk turns chia seeds into a simple, nutritious, and delicious breakfast pudding reminiscent of tapioca. Fresh berries add a burst of flavor and sweetness, while chopped pistachio nuts add a nice crunch.

SERVES: 4   **PREP TIME:** 5 mins , plus chilling   **COOK TIME:** none

INGREDIENTS

1 cup unsweetened almond milk

1 cup plain low-fat yogurt

2 tablespoons pure maple syrup

1½ teaspoons vanilla extract

pinch of salt

2 tablespoons chia seeds

1½ cups hulled and sliced strawberries

⅓ cup toasted pistachio nuts, chopped

maple syrup, for drizzling (optional)

1. Put the almond milk, yogurt, maple syrup, vanilla extract, and salt into a medium bowl and stir to combine.

2. Stir in the chia seeds and let stand for about 30 minutes at room temperature. Stir the mixture well to make sure the seeds are well incorporated, then cover and chill in the refrigerator for at least 8 hours or overnight.

3. To serve, spoon the pudding into serving bowls and top with the strawberries, nuts, and a drizzle of maple syrup, if using.

per serving: 190 cals / 8.9g fat / 1.4g sat fat / 21.8g carbs / 13.7g sugars / 5.7g fibre / 6.9g protein / 200g sodium

BUTTERNUT SQUASH & PECAN PANCAKES

Adding delicious nuts and nutrient-rich butternut squash—or other winter squash, such as acorn squash or pumpkin—to these mouthwatering pancakes gives them a real health boost. They make a great breakfast dish and are ideal for a leisurely weekend brunch.

SERVES: 6   **PREP TIME:** 15 mins   **COOK TIME:** 30 mins

INGREDIENTS

1 ¼ cups all-purpose flour

3 tablespoons chopped pecans

¼ cup firmly packed light brown sugar

2 teaspoons baking powder

½ teaspoon cinnamon

¼ teaspoon salt

1 egg

1 ¼ cups low-fat buttermilk

¾ cup peeled, cooked, and mashed butternut squash, pumpkin, or other winter squash

1 teaspoon vanilla extract

1 spray vegetable oil spray

½ cup maple syrup, to serve

1. In a medium bowl, combine the flour, nuts, sugar, baking powder, cinnamon, and salt. In a large bowl, whisk together the egg, buttermilk, squash, and vanilla extract. Beat the dry mixture into the wet mixture until combined.

2. Spray a nonstick skillet with the oil spray and heat over medium–high heat. When the pan is hot, ladle in the batter, ¼ cup at a time, to make 3¾–4-inch pancakes.

3. Cook for 2–3 minutes or until bubbles begin to burst in the tops of the pancakes and they are lightly browned on the bottom. Flip over and cook for an additional 2 minutes, until lightly brown on the other side. Serve immediately with maple syrup.

TIP: *Substitute the all-purpose flour with whole-wheat flour to increase the fiber content.*

per serving: 228 cals / 4.5g fat / 0.8g sat fat / 43.7g carbs / 28g sugars / 0.6g fibre / 6g protein / 240g sodium

BANANA, GOJI & HAZELNUT BREAD

On mornings when you don't have time to eat breakfast before you leave for work, wrap a slice or two of this superfood-packed bread in parchment paper to eat when you get there.

MAKES: 10 slices   **PREP TIME:** 20 mins, plus cooling   **COOK TIME:** 1 hour

INGREDIENTS

6 tablespoons butter, softened, plus ½ tablespoon for greasing

½ cup firmly packed light brown sugar

2 eggs

3 bananas (about 1 pound), peeled and mashed

1 cup whole-wheat flour

1 cup all-purpose white flour

2 teaspoons baking powder

½ cup coarsely chopped unblanched hazelnuts

⅓ cup goji berries

⅔ cup dried banana chips

1. Preheat the oven to 350°F. Grease a 9 x 5 x 3-inch loaf pan and line the bottom and two long sides with parchment paper.

2. Cream the butter and sugar together in a large bowl. Beat in the eggs, one at a time, then mix in the bananas.

3. Put the whole-wheat flour, white flour, and baking powder into a bowl and mix well. Add to the banana mixture and beat until smooth. Add the hazelnuts and goji berries and stir well.

4. Spoon the batter into the prepared pan, smooth the top, then sprinkle with the banana chips. Bake in the preheated oven for 50–60 minutes, or until well risen, slightly cracked on top, and a toothpick comes out cleanly when inserted into the center.

5. Let cool for 5 minutes, then loosen the edges with a blunt knife and turn out onto a wire rack. Let cool completely, then peel away the paper. Store in an airtight container for up to 3 days.

TIP: *Naturally rich in fruit sugar and starch, bananas are an energy-boosting food. They have plenty of potassium, helping to regulate blood pressure and lower the risk of heart attacks and strokes. They also contain the amino acid tryptophan and vitamin B6, which help in the production of mood-boosting serotonin.*

---

per slice: 276 cals / 10g fat / 2.5g sat fat / 43g carbs / 19g sugars / 3.5g fibre / 5.5g protein / 320g sodium

LUNCH & DINNER

SPICY PEANUT SOUP

This spicy and satisfying soup gets rich flavor from peanut butter and a kick from herbs and chiles. Serve it with hunks of home-style bread for dunking, or over steamed rice.

SERVES: 4   **PREP TIME:** 15 mins   **COOK TIME:** 35–40 mins

INGREDIENTS

1 tablespoon vegetable oil

1 small onion, chopped

1 tablespoon finely chopped fresh ginger

2 garlic cloves, finely chopped

½ teaspoon ground cumin

½ teaspoon black pepper

¼ teaspoon ground cinnamon

¼ teaspoon cayenne pepper

¼ teaspoon turmeric

1½ teaspoons salt

2–4 serrano chiles, finely chopped

2½ cups peeled and diced sweet potatoes

3 cups vegetable broth

1 (14½-ounce) can diced tomatoes, with their juices

½ cup smooth peanut butter

½ cup coconut milk

juice of 1 lemon

2 tablespoons chopped fresh cilantro leaves

2 scallions, thinly sliced, and chopped fresh cilantro leaves (optional) to garnish

1. Heat the oil in a medium saucepan over medium heat. Add the onion and sauté, stirring frequently, for 10 minutes, until soft. Stir in the ginger, garlic, cumin, black pepper, cinnamon, cayenne pepper, turmeric, and salt.

2. Add the chiles, sweet potatoes, and broth and increase the heat to medium–high. Bring the mixture to a boil, then reduce the heat to medium–low and simmer for 20 minutes, until the sweet potatoes are tender.

3. Add the tomatoes with their can juices and the peanut butter. Puree the soup in a blender. Return the soup to the pan and stir in the coconut milk, lemon juice, and cilantro. Heat over medium heat until heated through. Serve hot, garnished with the scallions and chopped cilantro, if using.

per serving: 402 cals / 26.6g fat / 9.2g sat fat / 34.9g carbs / 13.3g sugars / 5.8g fibre / 11.7g protein / 1800g sodium

1

2

3

CARROT & ALMOND SOUP

This smooth and comforting soup is a classic pairing combining the antioxidant power of carrots with the vitamin-boosting benefits of the almond. Ultimately, though, this is a delicious soup that will tempt even the fussiest of palates.

SERVES: 4   PREP TIME: 15 mins   COOK TIME: 30 mins

INGREDIENTS

2 tablespoons olive oil

1 yellow onion, diced

2 garlic cloves, minced

8 carrots (about 1 pound), sliced

1 teaspoon salt

1½ teaspoons ground cumin

½ teaspoon ground coriander

½ teaspoon black pepper

½ teaspoon cayenne pepper

1 teaspoon sweet paprika

¼ teaspoon ground ginger

5 cups chicken broth

⅓ cup blanched almonds

8 ounces Spanish chorizo, diced

½ cup slivered almonds

juice of 1 lemon

⅓ cup coarsely chopped fresh cilantro leaves

1. Put the oil into a large saucepan and heat over medium–high heat. Add the onion and garlic and cook for 5 minutes, stirring frequently, until the onion is soft. Add the carrots, salt, cumin, ground coriander, black pepper, cayenne pepper, paprika, and ginger and cook, stirring, for another minute. Add the broth and blanched almonds and bring to a boil. Reduce the heat to low and simmer, uncovered, for about 20 minutes, until the carrots are soft.

2. Meanwhile, heat a heavy skillet over medium–high heat. Add the diced chorizo and cook for 6–8 minutes, stirring frequently, until the fat begins to render and the meat begins to brown. Add the slivered almonds and continue to cook, stirring frequently, until the meat is brown and the almonds are golden and crisp. Transfer to a plate lined with paper towels to drain.

3. Puree the soup with a handheld blender until smooth. Bring to a simmer over medium heat, then stir in the lemon juice and fresh cilantro.

4. Serve the soup hot, garnished with the crispy chorizo and slivered almonds.

per serving: 492 cals / 42.4g fat / 11g sat fat / 12.7g carbs / 3g sugars / 3.4g fibre / 19.6g protein / 2,720g sodium

CURRIED CHICKEN SALAD WRAPS

This chicken salad is dressed up with spicy curry powder, creamy mayonnaise, sweet raisins, and crunchy pecans. Wrapped in warmed tortillas, this makes a delicious and filling lunch.

SERVES: 4   **PREP TIME:** 5–8 mins   **COOK TIME:** 10 mins

INGREDIENTS

4 flour tortillas

3 cups diced or shredded cooked chicken

⅓ cup mayonnaise

1 teaspoon Dijon mustard

½ teaspoon salt

2 tablespoons curry powder

⅓ cup raisins

⅓ cup toasted unsalted cashew nuts, coarsely chopped

4 large lettuce leaves

1. Preheat the oven to 400°F.

2. Wrap the tortillas in aluminum foil and heat in the preheated oven for about 10 minutes.

3. Meanwhile, put the chicken, mayonnaise, mustard, salt, curry powder, raisins, and nuts into a medium bowl and stir until well combined.

4. Divide the chicken mixture among the warmed tortillas, add a lettuce leaf to each, and roll up, folding up the ends of the tortillas to hold in the filling. Serve immediately.

> **TIP:** *This is a great way to use up leftover roasted chicken, turning a delicious Sunday dinner into an enviably delicious weekday lunch.*

per serving: 489 cals / 21.2g fat / 4.6g sat fat / 43.8g carbs / 11.9g sugars / 3.5g fibre / 31.7g protein / 720g sodium

PEAR, CELERY, BLUE CHEESE & WALNUT SALAD

Spinach is a veritable nutritional powerhouse—it has long been associated with energy renewal, and its rich iron content improves the quality of red blood cells. Combining it with ripe pears, walnuts, and soft blue cheese creates a real treat of a salad.

SERVES: 2 **PREP TIME:** 25 mins **COOK TIME:** none

INGREDIENTS

4 celery stalks

1 large juicy pear, such as Bartlett

lemon juice

3 tablespoons chopped fresh flat-leaf parsley

pinch of sea salt

3 cups arugula

½ bunch of watercress or 2 cups of other peppery greens

4 ounces blue cheese, broken into small chunks

¼ cup coarsely chopped walnuts

DRESSING

1 large, juicy pear, such as Bartlett

1 tablespoon lemon juice

¼ cup walnut oil

¼ teaspoon pepper

pinch of sea salt

1. Trim the celery and remove the strings with a swivel peeler. Slice into bite-size pieces. Put into a shallow bowl.

2. Quarter and core the pear but do not peel. Slice each quarter lengthwise into thin segments. Add to the celery. Sprinkle with a little lemon juice to prevent discoloration.

3. To make the dressing, quarter and core the pear. Slice one quarter lengthwise into thin segments. Add to the pear slices in the bowl. Peel and coarsely chop the remaining pear quarters.

4. Process the chopped pear and the remaining dressing ingredients with an immersion blender for 30 seconds, or until smooth. Scrape into a small bowl.

5. Toss the celery and pears with about ⅓ cup of the dressing, or enough to just coat. Stir in the parsley. Season with the salt.

6. Arrange the arugula and watercress on individual plates. Arrange the pear and celery mixture on top. Sprinkle with the cheese and nuts. Spoon the remaining dressing over the salad and serve.

per serving: 419 cals / 27.5g fat / 9.7g sat fat / 34.3g carbs / 20.4g sugars / 7.4g fibre / 13.2g protein / 520g sodium

RED CABBAGE WITH NUTS, MUSHROOMS & BACON

Hazelnuts have significant health benefits—they are rich in dietary fiber, vitamins, and minerals and are packed with phytochemicals, which offer multiple health-giving properties. They also have a pleasant sweet taste when served in a salad such as this one.

SERVES: 4   **PREP TIME:** 10 mins   **COOK TIME:** 35 mins

INGREDIENTS

½ head of red cabbage

2 tablespoons canola oil

6 thin bacon strips, chopped

1 onion, chopped

2 teaspoons thyme leaves

2 cup coarsely chopped cremini mushrooms

½ cup toasted hazelnuts, chopped

grated zest of 1 lemon

1 teaspoon sea salt flakes

½ teaspoon pepper

½ teaspoon sugar

2 tablespoons apple cider vinegar

1 cup beef broth

¼ cup chopped fresh parsley

pat of lightly salted butter, to serve

1. Cut the cabbage into quarters lengthwise, discarding the tough core in the center. Slice the leaves widthwise into ribbons.

2. Heat the oil in a flameproof casserole dish over medium–high heat. Add the bacon and cook for about 5 minutes, until crisp.

3. Reduce the heat to medium, add the onion and thyme, and sauté for 5 minutes, until the onion is translucent. Add the mushrooms and cabbage and sauté for an additional 5 minutes, until starting to soften.

4. Stir in the nuts, lemon zest, salt, pepper, and sugar and cook for an additional 3 minutes. Pour in the vinegar and broth, cover, and bring to a boil, then reduce the heat and simmer for 15 minutes, until the cabbage is tender.

5. Transfer to a warm serving dish. Stir in the parsley and butter, and serve immediately.

per serving: 386 cals / 32.4g fat / 10g sat fat / 15.6g carbs / 7g sugars / 4.5g fibre / 12.3g protein / 1,360 sodium

HAM & BRIE SANDWICHES WITH PISTACHIO SPREAD

The advantage of this pistachio tapenade is that once the figs are soft, you can just process the ingredients and it is ready. The tapenade can be combined with raw vegetables as a dip, mixed with penne pesto pasta, or used cold as a sandwich spread, as here.

SERVES: 4   **PREP TIME:** 10 mins   **COOK TIME:** 30 mins

INGREDIENTS

PISTACHIO SPREAD

½ cup quartered dried figs

½ cup pitted kalamata olives

½ cup roasted, unsalted pistachio nuts

grated zest and juice of 1 lemon

2 teaspoons capers, drained

½ teaspoon pepper

SANDWICHES

1 French bread, cut into 4 pieces and halved

4 ounces Brie, chilled and sliced

8 paper-thin slices prosciutto

1. To make the spread, put the figs into a small saucepan and add water just to cover. Bring to a boil over medium–high heat, reduce the heat to low, and simmer for 20–30 minutes, until the figs are soft and most of the water has evaporated.

2. Transfer the figs, along with any remaining liquid, to a food processor. Add the olives, pistachio nuts, lemon zest and juice, capers, and pepper and pulse to a chunky puree.

3. To make the sandwiches, spread one side of each French bread piece with about 2 tablespoons of pistachio spread. Divide the cheese evenly among the sandwiches. Top the cheese on each sandwich with two slices of prosciutto. Close up the sandwiches and serve at room temperature.

per serving: 458 cals / 21g fat / 7.5g sat fat / 47.5g carbs / 12.4g sugars / 5.4g fibre / 22.5g protein / 1,040g sodium

WARM QUINOA, ROASTED SQUASH & PINE NUT SALAD

Quinoa was considered a sacred food by the Incas, and has long been prized for its flavor and ability to keep you feeling full. Loaded with protein and vitamins, it is perfect for a salad.

SERVES: 2   **PREP TIME:** 20 mins   **COOK TIME:** 30 mins

INGREDIENTS

⅔ cup white quinoa, rinsed

1½ cups cold water

1½ cups bite-size butternut squash, acorn squash, pumpkin, or other winter squash chunks

¼ cup olive oil

pinch of cayenne pepper

pinch of salt

3 tablespoons pine nuts

½ cup coarsely chopped fresh flat-leaf parsley

¾ cup baby spinach

juice of ¼ lemon

salt and pepper (optional)

1. Preheat the oven to 350°F. Put the quinoa into a saucepan. Add the water, bring to a boil, then cover and simmer over low heat for 10 minutes. Remove from the heat, but leave the pan covered for an additional 7 minutes to let the grains swell. Fluff up with a fork.

2. Meanwhile, put the squash and 2 tablespoons of the oil into a large roasting pan, sprinkle with the cayenne pepper and salt, and toss well. Roast in the preheated oven for 25 minutes, or until crisp on the edges and tender. Transfer to a large bowl.

3. Toast the pine nuts in a dry skillet over high heat until they are light brown, then put them into the bowl. Gently mix in the quinoa, parsley, and spinach, being careful that nothing breaks up, then season with salt and pepper, if using.

4. Divide the salad between two plates, and drizzle with the remaining oil and the lemon juice.

per serving: 521 cals / 37g fat / 4.5g sat fat / 40.5g carbs / 2.0g sugars / 4.6g fibre / 9.9g protein / 600g sodium

ALMOND MILK

Almond milk is a healthy alternative to cow milk for many reasons. For one thing, it's low in fat and calories. It's also a great source of the antioxidant vitamin E, which helps to prevent cancer and premature aging, and of many other vitamins and minerals, such as copper, zinc, iron, magnesium, manganese, calcium, phosphorus, potassium, and selenium. Flavonoids in almond milk also help fight free radicals in the body, thereby protecting you from various degenerative diseases, such as osteoporosis and type-2 diabetes. Almond milk is free from both cholesterol and saturated fat and is high in omega-3 fatty acids, which help lower cholesterol and protect the heart.

You can use almond milk in the same way that you would use cow milk; put it in your coffee or tea, pour it over cereal, use it as a substitute for cow milk in recipes, or drink it straight out of a glass (we recommend that you accompany it with a cookie!).

Almond milk is easy to make at home—and making your own is considerably less expensive than buying it. Better still, while store-bought almond milk is often loaded with sweeteners, preservatives, thickeners, and other additives, homemade almond milk is made with nothing but raw almonds and water. This plain version is delicious on its own and is perfect for using in our recipes instead of using store-bought almond milk, but you can also add natural sweeteners (honey, sugar, maple syrup, agave syrup, or stevia) or spices (cinnamon or vanilla extract) to turn it into a sweet treat in its own right.

2

3

HOW TO MAKE ALMOND MILK

INGREDIENTS

1 cup raw almonds

2 cups water, plus extra for soaking

1. Put the almonds into a medium bowl and cover with 1 inch of water. Soak overnight and then drain, discarding the soaking water.

2. Put the almonds into a blender with the water and process until the nuts are pulverized.

3. Strain the mixture through cheesecloth into a bowl or jar, squeezing out as much liquid as you can. Discard the solids. The almond milk can be used immediately or stored in a covered container in the refrigerator for up to a week.

CHICKEN & PEANUT CURRY

If you like warmth and an element of spice in your meals, then here is a dish offering the magical combination of chicken, peanuts, and spices.

SERVES: 4   **PREP TIME:** 15 mins   **COOK TIME:** 20 mins

INGREDIENTS

½ cup roasted, unsalted peanuts

4 skinless, boneless chicken breasts, halved

1 tablespoon vegetable oil

1 shallot, diced

2–4 tablespoons Thai red curry paste

1 (14-ounce) can coconut milk

1 tablespoon Thai fish sauce

1 tablespoon packed light brown sugar

juice of 1 lime

½ cup chopped fresh cilantro leaves, plus a few cilantro sprigs to garnish (optional)

freshly cooked long-grain rice, to serve

1. Put the peanuts into a food processor and process for 2–3 minutes, until they form a smooth butter.

2. Line a large steamer basket with parchment paper and put the chicken breasts onto the paper. Place the steamer over boiling water, cover, and steam for 10–12 minutes, until the chicken is tender and there is no sign of pink when cutting through the thickest part of the meat.

3. Meanwhile, heat the oil in a large skillet and add the shallot. Cook, stirring frequently, for 5 minutes, or until soft. Add the curry paste and cook, stirring, for an additional minute.

4. Open the can of coconut milk and scoop off the thick cream that has risen to the top. Add the cream to the pan and cook, stirring, until it begins to simmer. Add the remaining coconut milk along with the peanut butter, Thai fish sauce, and sugar. Bring to a boil, then reduce the heat to low. Simmer for 5 minutes, or until the sauce thickens.

5. Stir in the lime juice and cilantro. To serve, divide the chicken breasts among bowls of freshly cooked rice, top with a generous amount of the sauce, and garnish with cilantro, if using.

per serving: 795 cals / 41.4g fat / 22.2g sat fat / 62g carbs / 8.5g sugars / 5.7g fibre / 46.2g protein / 640g sodium

MACADAMIA-CRUSTED SALMON WITH PINEAPPLE SALSA

The tropical flavours of macadamia nuts, coconut, and pineapple make this simple salmon dish extra-special, and it's also a refreshingly easy dish to prepare.

SERVES: 4   **PREP TIME:** 20 mins, plus resting   **COOK TIME:** 10–15 mins

INGREDIENTS

1 tablespoon vegetable oil, for brushing

1 cup chopped, roasted, unsalted macadamia nuts

½ cup panko bread crumbs

2 tablespoons all-purpose flour

4 tablepoons unsalted butter, melted

4 salmon fillets (about 6 ounces each)

1 teaspoon salt

½ teaspoon pepper

2 tablespoons coconut milk

SALSA

2 cups chopped pineapple

½ red onion, diced

2 jalapeño chiles, seeded and finely chopped

¼ cup fresh finely chopped cilantro

½ teaspoon salt

juice of 1 lime

1 tablespoon olive oil

1. Preheat the oven to 425°F and line a baking sheet with parchment paper. Brush the paper with the oil.

2. Put the nuts, bread crumbs, flour, and butter into a medium bowl and stir to mix well.

3. Season the salmon fillets on both sides with the salt and pepper and place them on the prepared baking sheet. Brush the tops of the fillets with the coconut milk. Top each fillet with one-quarter of the nut-and-bread-crumb mixture, pressing it into the fish in an even layer.

4. Bake the coated fish in the preheated oven for 10–15 minutes, or until the topping is golden brown and the fish is cooked and flakes easily with a fork.

5. Meanwhile, make the salsa. Put all of the ingredients into a bowl and stir together until well combined.

6. Remove the fish from the oven and let rest for a few minutes. Serve hot, topped with the pineapple salsa.

per serving: 927 cals / 72g fat / 19.1g sat fat / 34.5g carbs / 11.9g sugars / 8.5g fibre / 38.4g protein / 1.6g sodium

2

3

5

PISTACHIO-CRUSTED LAMB CHOPS

*Chopped pistachios and garlic make a tasty, crunchy coating for meaty lamb chops.
A sauce of sweet dried cherries and ruby port makes this an elegant dinner-party dish.
Serve the chops on a bed of creamy polenta for an extra-special touch.*

SERVES: 4   **PREP TIME:** 20 mins, plus resting   **COOK TIME:** 40 mins

INGREDIENTS

2 tablespoons olive oil

½ onion, thinly sliced

1 cup ruby port

1 cup dried sweet cherries,
coarsely chopped

1 cup chicken broth

1 tablespoon honey

1¾ teaspoons salt

3 garlic cloves

¾ cup roasted, unsalted
pistachio nuts

8 lamb chops

½ teaspoon pepper

1 tablespoon Dijon mustard
mixed with 1 tablespoon
water

1. Preheat the oven to 425°F.

2. Heat the oil in a heavy skillet over medium-high heat. Add the onion and cook for about 5 minutes, stirring occasionally, until soft. Add the port, cherries, broth, honey, and ¾ teaspoon of the salt and bring just to a boil. Reduce the heat to medium–low and simmer for about 20 minutes, until the sauce is thick and syrupy.

3. Meanwhile, put the garlic into the food processor and pulse until finely chopped. Add the nuts and pulse until finely chopped. Transfer to a plate.

4. Season the lamb chops on all sides with the remaining salt and the pepper, then brush with the mustard mixture. Press each lamb chop into the nut mixture to coat well all over.

5. Transfer the chops to a baking sheet and bake in the preheated oven for 6 minutes. Turn over and cook for an additional 6 minutes for medium–rare, or 7–8 minutes for well-done. Remove from the oven and loosely tent with aluminum foil. Let rest for 5 minutes before serving.

6. Serve hot, with the sauce spooned over the top.

per serving: 859 cals / 47.1g fat / 16.2g sat fat / 50g carbs / 29.4g sugars / 11.7g fibre / 43.4g protein / 1,400g sodium

ROASTED NUT LOAF

The benefit of a nut roast is that you can make it in advance, reducing the preparation if you are planning to serve it with all the standard roast trimmings. The dish can also be served cold with a crispy salad, in sandwiches, or with a warming bowl of soup.

SERVES: 6   **PREP TIME:** 20 mins   **COOK TIME:** 35–40 mins

INGREDIENTS

1 tablespoon olive oil, for brushing

2 tablespoons olive oil

1 large onion, finely chopped

1 cup ground almonds (almond meal)

¾ cup finely chopped cashew nuts

1 cup fresh whole-wheat bread crumbs

½ cup vegetable broth

finely grated zest and juice of 1 small lemon

1 tablespoon finely chopped rosemary leaves

salt and pepper (optional)

fresh rosemary sprigs and lemon slices, to garnish (optional)

1. Preheat the oven to 400°F. Brush a 9 x 5 x 3-inch loaf pan with oil and line with parchment paper.

2. Heat the oil in a large saucepan, add the onion, and sauté over medium heat, stirring, for 3–4 minutes, until soft.

3. Stir in the almonds, cashew nuts, bread crumbs, broth, lemon zest and juice, and rosemary. Season with salt and pepper, if using, and stir well to mix.

4. Press the mixture into the prepared pan, brush with oil, and bake the loaf in the preheated oven for 30–35 minutes, until golden brown and firm.

5. Turn out and serve hot, garnished with rosemary sprigs, lemon slices, and pepper, if using.

per serving: 429 cals / 34.8g fat / 4.5g sat fat / 22.3g carbs / 5.4g sugars / 12.2g fibre / 0.3g protein / 2,000g sodium

CHICKPEA WALNUT PATTIES

These hearty patties are similar to falafel, but they have the added richness and flavor of walnuts. They are delicious served on toasted hamburger buns with lettuce, tomato, and mayonnaise or tahini sauce.

SERVES: 4   **PREP TIME:** 15 mins, plus chilling   **COOK TIME:** 10 mins

INGREDIENTS

2 garlic cloves

1 shallot

1 (15-ounce) can chickpeas, drained and rinsed

15 sprigs fresh flat-leaf parsley

1 teaspoon ground coriander

1 teaspoon ground cumin

½ teaspoon salt

⅛ teaspoon cayenne pepper

2 tablespoons olive oil

2 tablespoons all-purpose flour

½ teaspoon baking powder

½ cup roasted, unsalted walnuts, coarsely chopped

2 tablespoons sunflower oil, for frying

1. Put the garlic and shallot into a food processor and pulse to chop. Add the chickpeas, parsley, coriander, cumin, salt, cayenne pepper, olive oil, and flour and pulse to a chunky puree. Add the baking powder and pulse once to incorporate. Add the walnuts and pulse once to incorporate.

2. Shape the chickpea mixture into four equal patties, about 4 inches in diameter. Chill in the refrigerator for at least 30 minutes or overnight.

3. Heat the sunflower oil in a large skillet over medium–high heat. Add the patties and cook for 4–5 minutes on each side until golden brown. Serve hot.

per serving: 320 cals / 24.7g fat / 2.6g sat fat / 18.1g carbs / 3.5g sugars / 5.2g fibre / 7g protein / 360g sodium

1

3

5

BUTTERNUT SQUASH & CHESTNUT RISOTTO

This comforting dish is full of nutritious content—pumpkin has vital antioxidants and vitamins, and chestnuts offer minerals, vitamins, and phytonutrients.

SERVES: 4   **PREP TIME:** 20 mins   **COOK TIME:** 1 hour

INGREDIENTS

1 tablespoon olive oil

3 tablespoons butter

1 small onion, finely chopped

2½ cups diced butternut squash or other winter squash

20 chestnuts (about 8 ounces), cooked and shelled

1½ cups risotto rice

⅔ cup dry white wine

1 teaspoon crumbled saffron threads, dissolved in ¼ cup of the broth

4 cups simmering vegetable broth

salt and pepper (optional)

1 cup freshly grated Parmesan cheese, plus extra to serve (optional)

1. Heat the oil with 2 tablespoons of the butter in a deep saucepan over medium heat until the butter has melted. Stir in the onion and squash and cook, stirring occasionally, for 5 minutes, or until the onion is soft and starting to turn golden and the squash begins to brown.

2. Coarsely chop the chestnuts and add to the mixture. Stir thoroughly to coat.

3. Reduce the heat, add the rice, and mix to coat in oil and butter. Cook, stirring constantly, for 2–3 minutes, or until the grains are translucent. Add the wine and cook, stirring constantly, for 1 minute, until it has reduced.

4. Add the saffron liquid to the rice and cook, stirring constantly, until all the liquid has been completely absorbed.

5. Gradually add the simmering broth, a ladleful at a time, stirring constantly. Add more liquid as the rice absorbs each addition. Increase the heat to medium so that the liquid simmers. Cook for 20 minutes, or until all the liquid has been absorbed and the rice is creamy. Season with salt and pepper, if using.

6. Remove the risotto from the heat and add the remaining butter. Mix well, then stir in the cheese until it melts. Adjust the seasoning, if necessary. Spoon the risotto onto four warm plates and serve immediately, sprinkled with grated cheese, if using.

per serving: 602 cals / 20g fat / 10g sat fat / 81g carbs / 8g sugars / 5.4g fibre / 15.5g protein / 840g sodium

TAGLIATELLE WITH HAZELNUT PESTO

Fresh and light, this protein-packed vegetarian main meal is made in a matter of minutes.

SERVES: 4   **PREP TIME:** 5 mins   **COOK TIME:** 10–12 mins

INGREDIENTS

12 ounces dried tagliatelle

1 cup fresh or frozen fava beans

PESTO

1 garlic clove, coarsely chopped

½ cup hazelnuts

3½ cups arugula

¼ cup olive oil

salt and pepper (optional)

1. For the pesto, put the garlic, hazelnuts, arugula, and oil into a food processor and process to a coarse paste. Season with salt and pepper, if using.

2. Bring a large saucepan of water to a boil. Add the pasta, bring back to a boil, and cook for 8–10 minutes, or according to the package directions, until tender but still firm to the bite. Add the beans 3–4 minutes before the end of the cooking time.

3. Drain the pasta and beans well, then return them to the pan. Add the pesto and toss to coat evenly. Serve immediately.

per serving: 522 cals / 22g fat / 2.5g sat fat / 71g carbs / 3g sugars / 9g fibre / 15g protein / 40g sodium

1

2

3

BAKING & DESSERTS

CHOCOLATE-DIPPED CHERRY & PISTACHIO BISCOTTI

These crunchy biscotti, studded with green nuts and red cherries and draped in dark chocolate, make a festive addition to a cookie platter, or a lovely Christmas gift.

MAKES: 40 slices   **PREP TIME:** 25 mins, plus cooling   **COOK TIME:** 45 mins

INGREDIENTS

2 sprays nonstick cooking spray

2 cups all-purpose flour, plus 1 tablespoon for dusting

1 cup whole-wheat flour

¼ teaspoon salt

1 cup granulated sugar

3 eggs

2 tablespoons vegetable oil

1 tablespoon vanilla extract

¼ cup coarsely chopped dried cherries

½ cup roasted unsalted pistachio nuts

10 ounces semisweet chocolate, chopped

1. Preheat the oven to 350°F and line a large baking sheet with parchment paper. Spray the paper with cooking spray.

2. Put the all-purpose flour, whole-wheat flour, and salt into a mixing bowl. Put the sugar and eggs into a separate large mixing bowl and beat with a handheld electric mixer on high speed for 3–4 minutes, until the mixture is thick and pale yellow. Add the oil and vanilla extract and beat until incorporated. Add the dry mixture to the wet mixture and beat on low speed until just combined. Add the cherries and nuts and mix to incorporate. Divide the dough into two pieces and turn out onto the prepared baking sheet. Shape each piece of dough into a 10-inch loaf and flatten it to 1 inch, squaring off the edges with your hands.

3. Bake in the preheated oven for 25 minutes, or until light brown. Remove from the oven and let cool on the baking sheet for about 10 minutes. Meanwhile, reduce the oven temperature to 325°F.

4. Slice each loaf into twenty ½-inch-thick slices. Arrange cut side down on the baking sheet and return to the oven for 10 more minutes. Flip the slices over and bake for 10 minutes. Remove from the oven and let cool completely.

5. Put the chocolate into a heatproof bowl set over a saucepan of gently simmering water and heat until melted. Dip one side of each of the biscotti into the chocolate, then return to the baking sheet, setting the biscotti on the uncoated side, and let cool for 10–15 minutes, until the chocolate is set. Serve at room temperature.

per biscotti: 120 cals / 4.8g fat / 2g sat fat / 16.7g carbs / 7.3g sugars / 1.7g fibre / 2.4g protein / trace sodium

CHOCOLATE & ALMOND MINI CAKES

These delightful mini cakes have nuts both inside and out, with ground almonds mixed in the cake base and a sumptuous topping of butter, soft brown sugar, and flaked almonds.

MAKES: 12   **PREP TIME:** 15 mins, plus cooling   **COOK TIME:** 22–24 mins

INGREDIENTS

¾ cup ground almonds (almond meal)

½ cup all-purpose flour

½ cup unsweetened cocoa powder

1 teaspoon baking powder

¼ teaspoon salt

4 tablespoons unsalted butter, at room temperature

⅓ cup granulated sugar

2 teaspoons vanilla extract

2 eggs

¼ cup heavy cream

TOPPING

½ cup slivered almonds

1 tablespoon packed light brown sugar

1 tablespoon unsalted butter, melted

1. Preheat the oven to 350°F and line a 12-cup muffin pan with paper cupcake liners.

2. Put the ground almonds, flour, cocoa powder, baking powder, and salt into a medium bowl and stir to combine.

3. Put the butter and sugar into a large bowl and cream with a handheld electric mixer until light and fluffy. Add the vanilla extract and the eggs, one at a time, and beat on medium–high speed until combined. Add half of the flour mixture and beat on medium–high until incorporated. Scrape down the side of the bowl, add the cream, and beat to incorporate. Scrape down the side of the bowl again, add the remaining flour mixture, and beat on medium-high until incorporated.

4. Scoop the batter into the prepared pan, filling each paper liner about halfway.

5. To make the topping, put the almonds and sugar into a small bowl and stir to combine. Add the butter and mix well to combine.

6. Divide the topping mixture among the paper liners. Bake in the preheated oven for 22–24 minutes, or until a toothpick inserted into the center of a cake comes out clean. Remove from the oven and let cool in the pan for 1–2 minutes, then transfer to a wire rack and let cool completely. Serve at room temperature.

per cake: 181 cals / 13g fat / 4.8g sat fat / 14.3g carbs / 6.9g sugars / 2.3g fibre / 4.6g protein / 120g sodium

SUPERFOOD CHOCOLATE BARK

*The darker the chocolate, the less sugar and more cocoa butter it contains,
so choose chocolate with at least 70 percent cocoa solids.*

SERVES: 6   **PREP TIME:** 20 mins , plus setting   **COOK TIME:** 5 mins

INGREDIENTS

4 ounces bittersweet
chocolate, broken into pieces

8 Brazil nuts, coarsely
chopped

¼ cup coarsely chopped
unblanched almonds,

2½ tablespoons coarsely
chopped pistachio nuts

2 tablespoons coarsely
chopped dried goji berries

2 tablespoons coarsely
chopped dried cranberries

1 tablespoon chia seeds

1. Put the chocolate into a heatproof bowl set over a saucepan of gently simmering water and heat for 5 minutes, until melted.

2. Line a large baking sheet with nonstick parchment paper. Stir the chocolate, then pour it onto the paper and quickly spread it out to an 8 x 12-inch rectangle.

3. Sprinkle the Brazil nuts, almonds, pistachio nuts, goji berries, cranberries, and chia seeds over the top, then let set in a cool place.

4. To serve, lift the chocolate off the paper and break into shards. Store in a plastic container in the refrigerator for up to 3 days.

per serving: 227 cals / 15.7g fat / 5.3g sat fat / 17.7g carbs / 10.2g sugars / 5.1g fibre / 5.1g protein / trace sodium

BANANA & MACADAMIA NUT BREAD

Macadamia nuts bring a tropical twist to this banana bread. Served warm on its own or with a little butter, it makes a comforting snack or a hearty breakfast.

MAKES: 10 slices   **PREP TIME:** 15 mins, plus cooling   **COOK TIME:** 1 hour 5 mins

INGREDIENTS

½ tablespoon butter, for greasing

1 cup all-purpose flour

½ cup whole-wheat flour

1 teaspoon baking soda

pinch of salt

2–3 large, ripe bananas

½ cup granulated sugar

½ cup firmly packed light brown sugar

½ cup sunflower oil

2 eggs, beaten

1 teaspoon vanilla extract

½ cup coarsely chopped macadamia nuts,

1. Preheat the oven to 350°F and grease the sides and bottom of an 8 x 4-inch loaf pan. Line with parchment paper.

2. Put the all-purpose flour, whole-wheat flour, baking soda, and salt into a mixing bowl and stir well.

3. Put the bananas into a separate large mixing bowl and mash until smooth. Add the granulated sugar, brown sugar, and oil and beat with a handheld electric mixer until combined. Add the eggs and vanilla extract and beat on medium speed for 1 minute, until well combined. Stir in the nuts.

4. Add the flour mixture and stir to combine. Transfer the batter to the prepared pan and bake in the preheated oven for 55 minutes–1 hour, until the outside is brown and a toothpick inserted into the center of the loaf comes out clean.

5. Remove from the oven, transfer to a wire rack in the pan, and let cool completely. Remove from the pan, cut into slices, and serve.

per slice: 364 cals / 20.3g fat / 3.1g sat fat / 43.6g carbs / 25.3g sugars / 2.5g fibre / 4.3g protein / 200g sodium

GINGER, NUT & OAT COOKIES

Cookies warm from the oven make a great welcome for kids back from school or for guests. Keep the dough in the refrigerator and slice off as many disks as you need, then bake in a preheated oven for 15 minutes.

MAKES: 18   **PREP TIME:** 30 mins, plus chilling   **COOK TIME:** 12–15 mins

INGREDIENTS

1½ sticks unsalted butter, softened and diced, plus ½ tablespoons for greasing

½ cup firmly packed dark brown sugar

1-inch piece fresh ginger, peeled and finely chopped

1¼ cups whole-wheat flour

1 cup rolled oats

¾ cup coarsely chopped unblanched hazelnuts

¾ cup coarsely chopped unblanched almonds,

1. Put a sheet of parchment paper about 12 inches long onto a work surface.

2. Cream together the butter, sugar, and ginger in a large bowl. Gradually beat in the flour, then the oats, hazelnuts, and almonds, until you have a soft dough. Spoon the dough into a 10-inch line along the parchment paper, then press it into a 2-inch-diameter roll. Wrap in the paper and chill in the refrigerator for 30 minutes or up to 3 days.

3. When ready to bake, preheat the oven to 350°F. Grease two baking sheets with butter. Unwrap the cookie dough and slice off as many cookies as you require. Arrange on the baking sheets, leaving a gap between each cookie. Bake for 12–15 minutes, or until cracked and brown at the edges.

4. Let the cookies cool on the baking sheets for 5 minutes, then loosen and transfer to a wire rack to cool completely.

per biscuit: 186 cals / 12.7g fat / 5.4g sat fat / 16.6g carbs / 6.8g sugars / 2.2g fibre / 2.3g protein / trace sodium

CHOCOLATE & MACADAMIA "CUPOOKIES"

These delicious mouthfuls are a hybrid between a cupcake and a cookie, and make a nutty and tempting wholesome treat.

MAKES: 12   **PREP TIME:** 30 mins, plus cooling   **COOK TIME:** 20 mins

INGREDIENTS

6 tablespoons butter, at room temperature

¼ cup chunky peanut butter

⅓ cup firmly packed light brown sugar

2 eggs, beaten

1 cup whole-wheat flour

1 teaspoon baking powder

⅓ cup coarsely chopped macadamia nuts

12 macadamia nuts, to decorate (optional)

CHOCOLATE FROSTING

4 ounces bittersweet chocolate, broken into pieces

2 tablespoons butter, diced

2 tablespoons packed light brown sugar

¼ cup milk

1. Preheat the oven to 350°F. Line a 12-cup muffin pan with paper muffin cups.

2. Add the butter, peanut butter, and sugar to a large bowl or food processor and beat together until light and fluffy.

3. Gradually beat a little of the egg into the butter mixture, alternating with a few spoons of the flour, then continue until all the egg and flour have been added and the batter is smooth. Beat in the baking powder and chopped nuts.

4. Divide the batter among the paper cups and bake in the preheated oven for 15 minutes, until risen, golden brown, and the tops spring back when lightly pressed with a fingertip. Let cool in the pan for 10 minutes.

5. To make the frosting, put the chocolate, butter, sugar, and milk into a heatproof bowl set over a saucepan of gently simmering water and heat, stirring occasionally, for 5 minutes, or until smooth.

6. Spoon the frosting over the cakes to cover them completely, then top each with a macadamia nut, if using. Leave in a cool place for 30 minutes to cool completely. Remove from the pan and serve. Store any leftovers in a plastic container in the refrigerator for up to 1 day.

per cookie: 274 cals / 19.2g fat / 8.3g sat fat / 22.3g carbs / 12.3g sugars / 2.9g fibre / 5.4g protein / 80g sodium

2

4

5

CHOPPING, GRINDING & TOASTING

CHOPPING NUTS

To chop small quantities of nuts, the best method is the simplest—a knife and some elbow grease. Put the nuts onto a cutting board. Hold the knife handle firmly with your dominant hand, and grasp the tip of the blade with your other hand. Rock the knife back and forth across the nuts until you've achieved the desired size. For larger quantities of nuts, pulsing them in a food processor works best and saves on effort.

GRINDING NUTS

When grinding nuts for baking recipes, there is always a danger of turning your nuts to butter, but there are a few tricks you can use to prevent tragedy. First, make sure that all of your food processor's parts— especially the bowl and blade—are completely dry and cool. The nuts themselves should be at room temperature. Put the nuts into the food processor and pulse, scraping down the side of the bowl every now and then, until you achieve the desired consistency. It's important that you pulse instead of using a steady processing setting to get the right consistency.

TOASTING NUTS

When cooking with nuts, toasting them first may seem redundant, but it's well worth the effort. Toasting nuts brings out their deep, earthy flavor and sweetness. It also gives them added crunch.

There are multiple methods for toasting nuts, so you can pick the one that works best for you.

IN THE OVEN

Preheat the oven to 350°F and spread out the nuts on a large baking sheet in a single layer. Bake the nuts, shaking the pan once in a while, until they are light golden brown and glossy (this will take anywhere from 5 minutes for small nuts, such as pine nuts, to 25 minutes for large nuts, such as chestnuts); check often because they will burn easily.

ON THE STOVE

Heat a large skillet over medium–high heat. Add the nuts in a single layer. Cook, stirring frequently, until you begin to smell a toasty, nutty aroma and the nuts are light golden brown (this will take anywhere from 5 minutes for small nuts, such as pine nuts, to 25 minutes for large nuts, such as chestnuts). Transfer the nuts from the hot pan to a plate or bowl as soon as they reach the toasted stage, because they can burn quickly.

IN THE MICROWAVE

The microwave is a great solution when you are pressed for time, although the nuts will not become as wonderfully browned as they will if you use either the stove or oven methods. To toast nuts in the microwave, spread them in a single layer in a microwave-safe dish. Cook on High for 1 minute at a time, stirring in between, until the nuts begin to smell toasted and turn crisp. This will take from 2–6 minutes, depending on the type of nuts you are toasting and how powerful your microwave is.

2

3

4

CHOCOLATE CREAM PIE WITH PECAN PASTRY

Pecan nuts, plain chocolate, and coconut cream are the key ingredients of this rich and tempting dessert. The mouthwatering pastry made from pecans, sugar and butter.

SERVES: 12   PREP TIME: 45 mins, plus cooling & chilling   COOK TIME: 15 mins

INGREDIENTS

PASTRY DOUGH

1¾ cups pecan pieces

¼ cup sugar

4 tablespoons butter, melted

FILLING

⅔ cup sugar

¼ cup cornstarch

½ teaspoon salt

4 extra-large egg yolks

3 cups almond milk

1 teaspoon vanilla extract

4 ounces semisweet chocolate, melted

3 ounces bittersweet chocolate, melted

TOPPING

1 (14-ounce) can coconut milk, chilled in the refrigerator overnight

1 tablespoon sugar

1 teaspoon vanilla extract

1. To make the dough, preheat the oven to 400°F.

2. Put the nuts and sugar into a food processor and pulse until the nuts are finely chopped. Add the butter and pulse to combine. Turn out the mixture into a 9-inch pie plate and press it evenly over the bottom and halfway up the side of the plate. Bake in the preheated oven for about 15 minutes, until light brown. Remove from the oven, place the pie plate on a wire rack, and let cool completely.

3. For the filling, put the sugar, cornstarch, salt, and egg yolks into a medium saucepan and stir to combine. Put over medium–high heat and add the almond milk in a thin stream, whisking constantly. Bring just to a boil, then immediately reduce the heat to low and cook, whisking constantly, for an additional minute, or until the mixture thickens. Push the mixture through a fine-meshed strainer, then stir in the vanilla extract and melted chocolates. Cover with plastic wrap, pressing it onto the surface of the mixture to prevent a film from forming, and chill in the refrigerator for at least 2 hours.

4. Spoon the chilled filling into the pastry shell, cover with plastic wrap, and chill for at least 4 hours or overnight.

5. To make the topping, open the can of coconut milk and carefully scoop out the thick cream at the top. Using a handheld electric mixer with a whisk attachment, beat the coconut cream with the sugar for 8–10 minutes, until it holds stiff peaks. Add the vanilla extract and beat to incorporate. Spoon the whipped cream on top of the pie and chill in the refrigerator for at least 2 hours. Serve chilled.

per serving: 372 cals / 27.1g fat / 10.8g sat fat / 29.7g carbs / 21.6g sugars / 3.5g fibre / 4g protein / 160g sodium

BROWN SUGAR WALNUT CAKE

This simple but enticing cake is studded with crunchy toasted walnuts and gets a deep, caramel-like flavor and a deliciously chewy crust from the brown sugar.

SERVES: 12   **PREP TIME:** 15 mins   **COOK TIME:** 1 hour 10 mins

INGREDIENTS

2 sticks butter, at room temperature, plus ½ tablespoons for greasing

2¼ cups all-purpose flour

½ teaspoon baking powder

½ teaspoon salt

2 cups firmly packed light brown sugar

¼ cup granulated sugar

1 tablespoon vanilla extract

4 eggs

¾ cup milk

½ cup chopped walnuts

1. Preheat the oven to 350°F and grease a 2½-quart tube pan.

2. Put the flour, baking powder, and salt into a medium bowl and mix to combine.

3. Put the brown sugar, granulated sugar, and butter into a separate bowl and beat with a handheld electric mixer for 4 minutes, or until pale and fluffy. Add the vanilla extract and mix to incorporate. Add the eggs, one at a time, beating well after each addition.

4. Add half the flour mixture and half the milk to the wet mixture and mix until just incorporated. Add the remaining flour and milk and mix until incorporated. Add the nuts and mix again until they are just incorporated.

5. Transfer the batter to the prepared pan and bake in the preheated oven for 1 hour–1 hour 10 minutes, or until a toothpick inserted into the middle of the cake comes out clean. Turn out the cake onto a wire rack and let cool completely before serving.

per serving: 449 cals / 21.4g fat / 11.2g sat fat / 59.6g carbs / 40.9g sugars / 1g fibre / 5.9g protein / 280g sodium

3

4

5

HONEYED CARROT & PECAN SQUARES

This cake is packed with vitamin A-boosting carrots, vitamin B- and mineral-boosting wheat germ, and energy-boosting whole-wheat flour.

MAKES: 15   **PREP TIME:** 25 mins, plus cooling   **COOK TIME:** 35 mins

INGREDIENTS

3 eggs

⅔ cup virgin olive oil

½ cup firmly packed light brown sugar

⅓ cup honey

1⅓ cups whole-wheat flour

¼ cup wheat germ

2 teaspoons baking powder

2 teaspoons ground ginger

grated zest of 1 orange, plus extra to decorate (optional)

1¼ teaspoons ground allspice

3 carrots, shredded

½ cup pecan pieces, plus extra to decorate (optional)

FROSTING

½cup plain Greek-style yogurt

⅔ cup cream cheese

1. Preheat the oven to 350°F. Line an 11 x 7-inch nonstick roasting pan with parchment paper, snipping into the corners diagonally, then pressing the paper into the pan so that both the bottom and sides are lined.

2. Crack the eggs into a large bowl, add the oil, sugar, and ¼ cup of the honey, and whisk until smooth. Put the flour, wheat germ, and baking powder into a small bowl, then add the ginger, orange zest, and 1 teaspoon of the allspice and stir. Add the dry ingredients to the egg mixture and beat again until smooth. Add the carrots and pecans and stir.

3. Spoon the batter into the prepared pan and spread it evenly over the bottom. Bake in the preheated oven for 30–35 minutes, or until well risen and a toothpick comes out cleanly when inserted into the center of the cake.

4. Remove the cake from the pan, peel off the parchment paper, and turn out onto a wire rack. Let cool.

5. To make the frosting, put the yogurt, cream cheese, and the remaining honey and allspice into a bowl and beat together until smooth. Spread the frosting over the cake, then sprinkle with nuts and orange zest, if using. Cut into 15 squares and serve.

per square: 294 cals / 20g fat / 5.3g sat fat / 25.8g carbs / 14.9g sugars / 2.4g fibre / 5.3g protein / 200g sodium

PISTACHIO ICE CREAM

Made in an electric ice-cream maker, with no dairy and no processed sugar, this is a treat you can truly feel good about. Creamy coconut milk and almond milk are sweetened with dates. Earthy pistachio nuts and almond extract give this an exotic and irresistible flavor.

SERVES: 6   **PREP TIME:** 10 mins , plus freezing   **COOK TIME:** none

INGREDIENTS

½ cup shelled unsalted pistachio nuts

1½ cups coconut milk

1½ cups almond milk

8–10 Medjool dates, pitted

1 teaspoon vanilla extract

½ teaspoon almond extract

1. Put the nuts and about ½ cup of the coconut milk into a food processor and process to a smooth paste.

2. Put the remaining coconut milk, the almond milk, dates, vanilla extract, and almond extract into a blender. Blend on high speed for 3–5 minutes, until pureed. Add the pistachio paste and process until well combined.

3. Transfer the mixture to the chilled container of an electric ice-cream maker and freeze according to the manufacturer's directions. The ice cream can be served immediately, or you can transfer it to a freezer-proof container and freeze overnight for a more solid consistency.

per serving: 195 cals / 7.5g fat / 1.8g sat fat / 31.6g carbs / 25.9g sugars / 4g fibre / 3.5g protein / 40g sodium

SUMMER FRUIT CRISP

Here you'll find three types of nuts combined in this delicious crumble topping, covering the warming, sweet mixture of tree and bush fruits, ranging from nectarines and plums to blackberries and cherries.

SERVES: 6   **PREP TIME: 15 mins, plus cooling**   **COOK TIME: 25 mins**

INGREDIENTS

FILLING

¼ cup firmly packed light brown sugar

1 tablespoon lemon juice

1 ½ teaspoons cornstarch

½ teaspoon vanilla extract

pinch of salt

2 large nectarines and/or peaches, pitted and sliced

6 plums and/or apricots, pitted and sliced

1 cup frozen blackberries and/or pitted cherry halves

TOPPING

⅓ cup toasted unsalted pecans

⅓ cup walnuts

⅓ cup almonds

⅔ cup firmly packed light brown sugar

½ cup rolled oats

⅓ cup all-purpose flour

pinch of salt

6 tablespoons chilled unsalted butter

1. Preheat the oven to 425°F.

2. To make the filling, put the sugar, lemon juice, cornstarch, vanilla extract, and salt into a large bowl and stir to mix well. Add the fruit and gently toss to coat. Transfer the fruit mixture to a 9-inch pie plate or baking dish and spread in an even layer.

3. To make the topping, put the pecans, walnuts, almonds, sugar, oats, flour, and salt into a food processor and pulse to combine. Add the butter and pulse until the mixture clumps into pea-size pieces. Spread over the fruit in an even layer.

4. Bake in the preheated oven for 20–25 minutes, until the topping is crisp and brown. Remove from the oven and let cool on a wire rack for 30 minutes before serving. Serve warm.

> **TIP:** *A crunchy topping crowns a mixture of seasonal fruit of your choice—apples and pears work, too. Serve with vanilla ice cream or whipped cream.*

per serving: 484 cals / 23.7g fat / 8.3g sat fat / 67.2g carbs / 49.8g sugars / 6.1g fibre / 6g protein / 200g sodium

RASPBERRY RICOTTA CHEESECAKE

Traditionally, cheesecakes have a crushed-cookie crust, but this granola-style crust is packed with delicious protein-filled nuts and crunchy cholesterol-lowering oats.

SERVES: 8   **PREP TIME:** 40 mins, plus soaking & chilling   **COOK TIME:** 15 mins

INGREDIENTS

1 tablespoon virgin olive oil, plus 1 tablespoon for brushing

2 tablespoons unsalted butter

⅓ cup maple syrup

½ cup rolled oats

⅓ cup coarsely chopped unblanched almonds

⅓ cup coarsely chopped unblanched hazelnuts

grated lemon zest, to decorate (optional)

maple syrup, to serve (optional)

TOPPING

¼ cup cold water

2½ teaspoons powdered gelatin

1 cup ricotta cheese

1 cup mascarpone cheese

1 cup plain yogurt

finely grated zest and juice of 1 unwaxed lemon

1 cup raspberries

1. To make the crust, preheat the oven to 325°F. Brush a 9-inch round, nonstick springform tart pan with a little oil. Put the butter, oil, and 2 tablespoons of the maple syrup into a saucepan over medium-low heat until the butter has melted. Remove the pan from the heat and stir in the oats and nuts.

2. Transfer the mixture to the prepared pan and press down into an even layer with the back of a fork. Bake for 15 minutes, or until golden, then let cool in the pan.

3. Meanwhile to make the topping, spoon the water into a small heatproof bowl, then sprinkle the gelatin over the top, making sure all the powder is absorbed. Let soak for 5 minutes. Place the bowl over a saucepan of gently simmering water until you have a clear liquid.

4. Put the ricotta cheese, mascarpone cheese, and yogurt into a bowl, spoon in the remaining maple syrup, and whisk until smooth. Mix in the lemon zest and juice, then gradually whisk in the gelatin mixture. Add half the raspberries and crush them into the mixture with a fork.

5. Spoon the topping onto the crust and smooth the surface. Sprinkle with the remaining raspberries. Cover and chill in the refrigerator for 4–6 hours, or until set.

6. To serve, run a knife around the edge of the pan, unclip and remove the springform, and slide the cheesecake onto a serving plate. Decorate with lemon zest, if using. Cut into wedges and drizzle with maple syrup, if using.

per serving: 389 cals / 29.3g fat / 14.3g sat fat / 22.9g carbs / 14.1g sugars / 3.2g fibre / 11g protein / 80g sodium

INDEX